# Baraka

*....a divine essence extended
from Spirit to the human consciousness*

# *Baraka*

*....a divine essence extended
from Spirit to the human consciousness*

## by John-Roger

I.S.B.N. 0-88238-961-0

First printing 1973
Copyright, © 1973, by
John-Roger

Revised edition 1982

Printed by Ambassador Printing Co., Inc.
711 Grandview Street, Los Angeles, California, 90057
United States of America

# Contents

# Introduction

We are all spiritual beings. We are all of God. There is nothing and no one that is not of God. The spark of God individualized within each human being is the Soul, which is the basic element of our existence. The Soul is forever connected to God. The connection is perfect and intimate; it is the source from which we draw our life. The nature and the essence of the Soul is *JOY*. It is joyful because it is of God and has knowledge of that.

The human consciousness is somewhat different. There are elements besides the Soul which make up the human consciousness. These elements can sometimes cloud the clarity of spiritual vision and interfere with our ability to perceive God directly. These elements are the body, imagination, emotions, mind, subconscious, and the unconscious.

The elements of human consciousness are actually microcosms of planes or realms of Light beyond the physical universe. Some realms are of a positive nature and others are of a negative nature. Much like the positive and negative polarities on a battery, the combination of positive and negative creates movement and action, the dynamics of "life" as we know it.

In the outer reality there are realms of existence which correspond to each level of consciousness present within the individual. The *physical* level of existence is obvious to all of us. It is the level of the physical universe which we can see. Corresponding to the imagination is the *astral* realm. Through our imagination on this plane, we give reality to our fantasies and scenes of our imagination. The *causal* plane of existence matches the emotional quality of the human consciousness. On this level our emotional creations come into a form of objective reality, to let us see their power. The *mental* realm corresponds to the mind, with all its confusions and doubts as well as its clarity and dynamic thrust. The *etheric* realm is the area where the power of our subconscious and unconscious becomes reality.

All of these levels are "negative" in nature -- not bad, but like the negative pole of a battery. Their influence will tend to keep us recycling within the lower worlds. Their power is designed to keep us on those levels. The Soul, however, is positive in nature. The realm of the Soul and the realms of Spirit above are designed to lift us up and bring us freedom. In the positive realms, the lower worlds lose their influence. The plan and purpose of the negative worlds becomes clear and in that clarity is freedom.

Let me give you an analogy of how the negative worlds function. Suppose you are walking on a mountain path, and "home" is about ten miles away. You set off on your journey, feeling good, and everything seems fine. Then you come to an area where the terrain gets very rough. There are a lot of trees down across the path; it's very steep. It becomes very foggy and rainy. It's hard to keep on the path. As you look for a way through, perhaps you scrape your leg or turn your ankle. The physical body gets cold and begins to ache. You feel tired and lose your enthusiasm for this journey. In your imagination, you start seeing the possibility that the entire ten miles is going to be like this. You start creating the image that it's never going to get any better, and you don't know how you'll ever make it home. Then the emotions come in with your imaginative scene, and you start feeling discouraged and depressed. You can't find a way around the trees, and in your imagination you've gone ahead of yourself and imagined the path isn't going to get any easier, so you start to cry. Then the mind may come into play and start thinking about another way to get home. Maybe it can't deal with the present situation, so it makes you believe that if you go in another direction entirely, you'll make it home. So you follow the new "direction" and turn away from the path that leads home. The unconscious level takes in all the data from all the other levels but doesn't have any tools to express on these other levels. It just stores the information and then feeds it back to you, so that every new turn in the path becomes an aspect of the last turn, and all sorts of vague fears and illusions come up to the surface of your consciousness. They frighten and confuse you and prevent you from seeing clearly what is really present for you in each moment of your journey.

As all of these aspects play back and forth in your consciousness, it becomes very easy to get lost, sidetracked, confused and frightened as you move through your experience, trying to find your way home. When you can reach beyond all these negative levels and perceive from the Soul, from the positive aspect of yourself, you can lift up in consciousness, see where your home is and see which path will lead you there. And whether the rough terrain lasts for ten miles or only a half mile, you can see what to do to traverse the path.

At that point, you can go back into your journey and use all the levels as tools to your advantage. You use your body to move through the space, toward your goal. You use your imagination to create the image of reaching home safely. You use your emotions to keep you happy and joyful. You use your mind to decide upon a good direction and keep you focused on completing that direction. And you use the areas of unconscious to strengthen you  as you learn to discern reality from illusion.

Into this matrix of life comes those who are enlightened, who have discovered how these different levels work and fit together, and who have experienced the Soul and Spirit directly. They are the ones we have called the masters and great teachers of mankind. They have assisted mankind to awaken to its greater destiny and taught of God's love and God's plan. Living in the higher realms of Light, they become imbued with the positive energy of Spirit. As they come into the lower worlds, they bring that energy to these levels. The Soul within each person intuitively recognizes that energy from Spirit as its greater reality and moves toward it. In this way we learn and grow in our awareness of God and are finally able to transcend the lower levels of consciousness and reach our home in God.

# Baraka

....a divine essence extended
from Spirit to the human consciousness

1

# The Master Forces

There are many levels of consciousness and many dimensions of space and time within many universes. The planet we call Earth is in only one of the many realms of Light. All consciousness, on all realms of Light including earth, is part of a greater order and plan of spiritual evolvement. The spiritual consciousness of humans extends into all realms, reaching from its home in the Soul realm down to the physical realm. In that sense, it exists on all realms simultaneously. But depending on the evolvement of the individual consciousness, a person's awareness of one realm may be greater than of another realm. Generally speaking, the human consciousness, dwelling in physical form, will have a much greater awareness of this earth plane and very little or no awareness of the higher realms.

There are, however, those people whose consciousnesses are more highly developed, whose spiritual evolvement is greater than the average, and who have a greater awareness not only of this physical realm, but also of the higher realms of Spirit. These are the great teachers, gurus and masters who come forward to teach and show the way to those who are ready to walk the spiritual path. Some are great masters who come from the lower realms of Light. Their messages can be very uplifting and inspiring; the abilities they demonstrate can be miraculous. Some are masters who bring forward a universal consciousness from higher, positive realms of pure Spirit. They have total awareness of all levels of consciousness and have the ability to work with, teach, guide, and show the way "home" to those Souls who are ready to break free from the cycle of reincarnation and return to the Soul realm.

Jesus the Christ was such a Master. And because he was so powerful and his impact on the Western world so great, those in the Western culture relate most readily to the Christ or the Christ consciousness as the manifestation of this higher level of spiritual consciousness and evolvement. Jews and Christians alike share in this tradition, and even though Jews do not recognize Jesus as the Messiah, the concept of the Messiah is a very important part of their tradition.

The Christ is a universal consciousness that dwells within everyone, although some are more awakened to and aware of it than others. The teachings of the Christ —not a church interpretation of Jesus' teachings—are universal; they do not conflict with any other teachings, but *encompass* all other teachings through their universal approach.

The consciousness of the Christ is the consciousness of pure Spirit, which exists within each man through the Soul. Spirit is the force which gives you your life, energy, and power. It's that spark of the divine which is the source of your "godness" or "goodness." The individual Soul of man exists as the indwelling Christ. But most people are imperfectly aware of the Christ within, so there is always at least one person on the planet who manifests the Christ through himself and comes forward to demonstrate outwardly that consciousness so that others may see and recognize that greater quality. The Christ within someone can awaken to the Christ within others. When they perceive the Christ consciousness, they begin to awaken to that greater expression in themselves.

There is a line of spiritual masters called "Mystical Travelers" who come directly through the line of the Christ into this planet. On other planets where the "Christ" is not the focus of universal spiritual force, the Mystical Traveler doesn't come through the line of the Christ. It may come through the All, the It of Itself, the Sarmad, or the Supreme God for which there is no name. The force which is the Supreme Lord of all universes is so omnipotent and so far beyond what the human mind can envision, there are no words which can describe or give sense to it. But when we speak using physical language, we must use words as reference points which have some meaning to most of us.

Those who have held the keys to the Mystical Traveler Consciousness in the past have brought to mankind the message of love, harmony, balance, honesty and integrity. Sometimes these spiritual messages have been given directly and openly, in a public way. Sometimes the Mystical Travelers live very quiet, ordinary lives. Some historical figures who have held the keys to the Traveler consciousness are Rama, Eli Hu, Jesus the Christ, and Huzur Maharaj Baba Sawan Singh, who taught the Sant Mat or Teachings of the Saints.

When we look back at the message of each one of these Travelers of Light and Sound, we are reminded that the message is always the same. The various messengers who bear the Light and Sound bring forward the same message time and again, because people continue to either forget or corrupt the message. Only a few individuals stand out as pinnacles of this Light force and let themselves be used as transformers to step down the spiritual energy so that it can be used on this physical realm. Each one who is divinely endowed with this knowledge comes to restate the ancient message and then to bring forward a special dispensation of that time and place it within the consciousness of men; this is the glory to which we are all heir.

At this time, right now, on the earth, the universal message is again being brought forward. Two thousand years ago, Jesus said, "He that believeth in Me, the works that I do shall he do also; and even greater works than these shall he do; because I go unto my Father." (John 14:12) What was this message? Was he speaking of his physical form? No, He was speaking from the spiritual consciousness. He was speaking from the Christ consciousness when He said, "I am the Alpha and the Omega." (Revelations 1:8) That's the Christ Spirit, which is in all of us.

Muhammad gave the message as the servant of God when he said that God is like all and God is among all. Then he proclaimed, "None exists but God." God constitutes the *whole being,* individually and collectively. Every Soul has the divine message within itself, not necessarily within the personality, mind or emotions, but within the *Self,* which is the same essence that Christians refer to as the Christ. The essence is the same, whatever tradition the words reflect. "There is no God but God" is again the message in this time. That was and will be the message. There is no other. You can be awakened to that realization when someone else speaks to you from the God-center, because that essence reaches in and stirs the same essence within you.

Now in this time, the Mystical Traveler again comes forward and says, "Yes, these promises have been given and these promises have been fulfilled." But the message also has been that in the latter days God would pour His Spirit out upon mankind and would make the heart which is hard become tender and loving. That is the message now, in this age.

We bring forward the close of one age; we unlock and fling open the doors to the New Age. The opportunity to transcend the physical realm and all the lower realms and move directly into Soul Consciousness is again being presented to those Souls who can recognize it. This is the work of the Movement of Spiritual Inner Awareness.  This is the work I have come to do. This is the message I bring you.

*2*

# *Baraka*

---

Part of my spiritual message comes on the frequency of certain words I use. There are two ancient words I use at the end of many of my seminars and Soul Awareness Discourses. Those words are *Baruch Bashan,* which means "the blessings already are." It is the statement that all the blessings which will ever be present exist here and now, and and all you have to do is move into the realization of those blessings. The frequency of those Hebraic words inherently conveys the blessings to your consciousness.

There is a line of ancient Masters of the Sufi tradition from which I am also descended, and in this line there is a word which is used mainly in an inner silence to invoke what could be called *virtue from heaven.* The word invokes a special protection and brings a special upliftment. The word is not as powerful as the words Baruch Bashan, but it is powerful. The word is *Baraka,* which represents a divine essence extended from Spirit to the human consciousness. Those people who have ascended into higher spheres or realms of Light receive of this essence, bring it forward into this level, and can bestow it upon others. You can read book after book after book and gain tremendous levels of information, but until you can find one who can bring *Baraka* to you, the information has been a waste of your time, in a sense of the word. If you receive *Baraka* and let it flow into you, it will flow through every center of your beingness and transform you as it uplifts you. *Baraka* is an essence of divine energy, divine love.

The experience of *Baraka* is described many ways. It is called the Holy Spirit, grace, "seeing the Light," and "hearing the Sound." *Baraka* is a universal experience. The symbology of this word is very interesting. It means taking from above and giving to above, taking from below and giving to above, taking from above and giving to below, and taking from below and giving to below. So as you receive, you give; as you give, you receive. Both actions exist simultaneously in a constant flow. Some people are busy just receiving. If this is what you do, the *Baraka* within you goes stale and stagnant. It is much like a river or stream flowing into a lake from which there is no outlet: the lake becomes brackish and dead. But if the stream flows into that which is continuously giving outward, then it always remains fresh and alive. In other words, when you do good works, Spirit, through its agent, continually delivers *Baraka* to you. When you feel you've "got it," "reached it," "don't need it any more," it will no longer be delivered to you. Then you will either have to manufacture it (which is difficult) or make it up (which is deceitful).

I don't like to speak of spiritual deceit, but there are those who will try to deceive you regarding spiritual issues. There are methods to test the Spirit so that you will not be pulled into areas of deceit. I'll tell you what they are and you can use them to test what I tell you. And if you don't find an attunement ringing with you, then maybe this is not for you. It's a way for you to know rather rapidly if these spiritual teachings are something within which you can work and live. It's very simple.

The way to test Spirit is as follows. Wherever you go, ask for God's Light to surround you, protect you and fill you. Place it ahead of you wherever you are going so that you will always be well received. And each time you meet somebody, ask this Light to be placed between you, not as a barrier, but as that which can clarify. When people speak to you, ask yourself, "Is this true for me?" You can't ask if it's true for everyone because there is no real truth for everyone, except God. Once you have found God, you have indeed found truth for everyone.

When you hear information being presented to you, place the Light between you and the speaker, as a channel for clear communication. Close your eyes for just a second and ask yourself, "If the information I am hearing is not true for me, I would like to be shown this in a clear way. And if this information is right for me, I would like to experience the presence of the Light and Spirit within me in an uplifting way." You will get feedback from Spirit if you ask for clarification in this way. You may feel goose pimples around the top of your head. You may feel a lift in energy. You may get a sensation of pulsation in the forehead. There are many, many ways that Spirit might signal you of its presence. If the situation is not right for you, you may get very restless and feel compelled to leave. Or you may get very sleepy and "drift off" for a few minutes. But you will have your answer, and you will know it. This is one way to decide the validity of what you hear.

Keep in mind that what may be valid for one person may not be valid for another; it is very well known that "one man's medicine is another man's poison." And it is very well known that we all must partake of life according to where we come from and where we are going, according to our life destinies. So you can't ask for the truth for a group; you can only ask for truth for yourself. You have a *right* to ask for the truth for yourself; you do not have the right to inflict your truth or preferences on others.

Some people have faithfully believed everything I've told them. And that's not the most beneficial way to run your life. That's not practical spirituality. When you hear any information, go home and contemplate it. See if there is a logic that works for you. Then see how it can work within your life, *if* it can work within your life. You might say, "I have a feeling this information wasn't meant for me because it doesn't apply to any of my situations." That may be a valid point of view. But a week from now, someone may come to you and say, "I have had this problem and don't know how to handle it," and you will remember the information that "wasn't for you," and say, "I think I have a suggestion or two for you." You relate the information, and they say, "Yes, that will work. I know that will clear it. Thanks a lot!"

These experiences are what we call the "miracles" of working with the Light. You allow yourself to be used as a channel for the Light. Information that might not do anything for you in a given moment may be very appropriate information in the future and allow you to be of service and assistance to someone else. The *Baraka* you received is then extended out to another, and the flow is continued.

Part of my job is to teach you to more effectively handle this physical level, so I show and tell you many techniques to overcome the forces of the negative worlds. A greater part of my job is to extend to you *Baraka,* the energy, force, and strength to overcome negativity and lift your consciousness into the positive. And an even greater part of my job is to work with you to establish you in Soul consciousness, in the realms of pure Spirit, so you will no longer be subject to patterns of reincarnation. The greatest joy you will experience is when you develop the ability to consciously transcend this physical form through Soul transcendence.

The *knowledge* of these higher realms is not enough, because you can "know" a lot of things without really *knowing* them. You can read what I have experienced and "know" it on an intellectual level, but until you have had the *experience,* the process may be much like a baby who sees the beam of a flashlight against a wall and goes to the wall to get the light. That beam is only a reflection of the light, not its source. Yet many of you do a similar thing: you go out into this land of reflected Light to see who will reflect Light back to you. It is a form of Light for which you are searching, yet you do not go for the source of the Light. Similarly, you may praise the color of a beautiful red wine but forget to check the color of the glass. Maybe the *glass* is red and the *wine* is white. So you continually fool yourself by gratifying your own illusion. This can cause pessimism and doubt to appear, and you miss the *Baraka* that is being continually extended to you. Confidence appears when you use your *experience* as your teacher.

There is also a knowing which doesn't necessarily come through experience, but through that inner conviction that just *knows*. Those of you who are men *know* you are men, and those of you who are women *know* you are women. You need no outside verification from any source other than yourself. You are what you are. That type of self-evident knowing sometimes appears inside of you when you are presented with spiritual teachings.

You *know* the truth of them. *Everything* being brought to you is *Baraka;* it is up to you to make all things *Baruch Bashan.* I will not attempt to change your attitudes; that is something you must change. That is your responsibility. I can extend to you a love that no one else can extend to you, a love which will not possess you or allow anything to harm you; this is also *Baraka.* This ancient Sufi word defies description and goes beyond vocabulary. It is pure essence of Spirit. It is the Source, not the reflection. The spiritual form I represent gets its power from the Source. It is an agent of the Supreme God. It is not reflection, although the physical form you see *is* reflection.

When people ask me "Are you John-Roger?" they are relating to the physical form, which is reflection. But I'll say "Yes," rather than, "No, this is just a physical form; the consciousness that is John-Roger is not this form." Such explanations can be very confusing to people who see only the three-dimensional world of reflected Light. The things you see and hear on this physical level are reflections of the Source. When you see the physical form of John-Roger or read or listen to my words, these are only reflections of the consciousness of *Baraka,* the *Baruch Bashan,* the Mystical Traveler/Preceptor, the force field called "John-Roger" or "J-R." This essence resides perfectly protected within each individual Soul. The physical manifestations are a mirror image of the greater reality, and as such, may be a distortion of the greater reality. And yet John-Roger is the physical form, also.

Let me say it to you this way: I am both in contact with the physical level of reality and the spiritual reality of the other realms simultaneously. By way of analogy, most human beings are like apples that have fallen from the tree (the Source) onto the ground. The Mystical Traveler is like an apple which has mainatained its connection to the tree, but the branch which holds the apple has bent over and reached all the way to the ground. So the apple is both on the ground with the other apples and still connected to the tree.

The Silent Ones, who are spiritual forces issuing forth out of the Sarmad, the Lord of the positive realms of Spirit, work directly in line with the energy of the Traveler in the Movement of Spiritual Inner Awareness. They are very difficult to find and identify for the simple reason that they are silent. To find them, you must be silent, also. People have asked me how often I am in contact with the Silent Ones, and I answer, "How often are you in contact with your eyes?" All the time. But when you look at something, do you see it or does your mind wander away from it so that you do not see? Contact with the Silent Ones is a similar process. By focusing there, I find that I have never left that greater consciousness. But because of the work that goes on in the three-dimensional level, there are times when I must turn my consciousness from the greater reality to answer questions like, "Should I wear red socks or blue ones?" or "Should I get another job, move to another city, and seek other friends?" Answering to this level is not usually of much value, but I will answer if the answer will ultimately lift you into a higher consciousness. So far, however, I haven't found anybody who profits much from the answers to those kinds of questions.

The work I do is much easier when you handle the "ten percent " level of the physical world as effectively as you can from your present level of knowledge and ability. You cannot have a hundred percent certainty regarding anything on this level, because you only have ten percent of your total awareness here. You do the best you can with the ten percent, and you work as closely to a hundred percent of your ten percent as possible. People who do their work to their full capacity of the ten percent have been called geniuses  Or sometimes they are called eccentrics because they are true to their own consciousness and not the world's opinions.

When you are true to yourself, you learn to maintain the dignity of your own divine consciousness so that, no matter what might be asked of you in moving your own spiritual inner awareness, whether by your family, employers, friends, or myself, it will be your joy to do what is asked. It will be an express on and manifestation of _Baraka._ And you will bypass the concerns of "what other people might say or think" and move into _doing._ If you do not have an attunement with Spirit, you will not find yourself experiencing _Baraka,_ no matter how much your mind says you are. If you have an attunement with Spirit, there is no task too big or too small to share divine love with others. You might find yourself tying a child's shoelaces, cleaning out a friend's garage, giving up your Saturday at the beach to help someone, doing your spiritual exercises, sending the Light to those who need your love and support, or any number of other things.

Once when I was getting off an airplane, a little lady was trying to get off but having difficulty because part of her luggage was in the aisle. I could have just kept going like the other people, but it was a chance to share *Baraka.* So I reached down, picked up her case, handed it to her, then waited until she could collect her things and step out into the aisle. She started glowing; the irritation that could have blocked her left, and she was clear. An acquaintence of mine happened to be on the same plane and saw this, and she thought it was wonderful that I would help this lady with her luggage, wait for her to go ahead of me, and go much slower in order to assist her. But the sharing of *Baraka* was my pleasure.

The only thing I ask of people is that they unfold into greater spiritual consciousness and share their awakening with more and more people. People have offered to do many things for me on this physical level; I do not require great assistance on this level. I ask only that you gain your *greater* spiritual awareness; that is what you can do for me. It is all I ask of you. And I will do whatever I can to assist you in that process of transcendence.

Too often people want to be the "teacher" to those around them, to be the "great spiritual saviour" and lead the mass exodus to Venus. All that may be okay if you want to stay in a three-dimensional realm. But if you're going to "lead the mass exodus" into the spiritual realms, you'd better first learn how to drive the bus, punch and collect the tickets, travel the correct routes, and keep your group together — because there are more Souls on the other realms of Light than there are here in the three-dimensional world. There is nothing to fear, but if you don't know your way, you can certainly find yourself at a loss.

Make sure that through your words and personality you don't overstep your spiritual ability. Be honest with yourself and others. If you have a little knowledge, let them know what your limits are. It's very probable that you can assist people by simply being who you are. And if they know what to expect, they will learn and grow from what you can share with them and bless you for it. But if you create a false impression of being more than you are, you will fall short of their expectations, and they may curse you for it. Be honest with yourself and others. It's an important key to your success. When you are freely sharing who you are, you allow *Baraka* to flow through you to them, and everyone participates in the blessings.

Some people say they don't know how far to go in sharing verbally with other people the ideas they've learned through MSIA® . But you can present information to people as you understand it without judging them by trying to determine beforehand what they can or cannot understand. And when you talk to them, you can say, "I don't know how much of this you want to hear. So when you've heard enough, just tell me or raise your hand and I'll stop." That's easy. But you don't even have to talk about the Light to share it with them. *Baraka can be shared silently.*

My staff and I were traveling on an airplane once, and a man sat down beside one of my staff members, who just turned and said, "Hi." It wasn't fifteen minutes before this man was telling us all the things he had experienced on his travels around the world. We just sat there and listened; this also was *Baraka.* Just listening to him and enjoying his trip vicariously was a way to share *Baraka* with him. He was a very perceptive seventy-one year old young man, and all of a sudden he started asking some very deep, penetrating questions: "What are you doing? What is this Movement you're part of? How does it work? What does it do? What is your purpose?" And when he was finished with the questions, the conversation shifted again to other things. That's one way to know when people have received the information they are searching for. A few minutes later this man asked, "May I have one of your business cards? I have a sister, and I think this is what she's been looking for." You might ask, "What about him? Didn't he want this for himself?" Does it really matter? This man *knew* what was going on. He had already made the contact and received *Baraka.*

That night the Mystical Traveler took this man into the inner realms and showed him many patterns; he accepted the Spirit. He knows what it is. He's not formally a member of MSIA®,  but he carries information and the spiritual energy to other people. He found out what worked. He recognized the validity of what we said. He said, "I'm seventy-one years old, but I never looked at life the way you do; that's really a very good way to look at it. In fact that makes life much more enjoyable and much more fulfilling."

One young man on my staff said to him, "Part of our philosophy is that since we're going to go through this life, we can go through it either laughing or crying. But we're going to go through it." The man said, "Yes! That's right!" At that time, my staff member was about twenty-two years old. Some people might see something awkward about a twenty-two year old man instructing a seventy-one year old man, but the man was much younger in terms of his openness. He wasn't "old" in the usual sense. He was alive and open, and it was so beautiful to share *Baraka* with him and so joyful when he began to share *Baraka* back with us. We were sharing Light, Spirit, the love of the Soul. As the sharing continued, other people came closer to share in this also. When the flight was over, we were no longer strangers to each other; certainly we didn't know each other intimately, but we did *know* each other. And that can be a blessing on this physical level.

# 3
# Twaji, the Gaze of God

Part of the coming together in brotherhood and sharing *Baraka* with one another involves the communication and connection that is transmitted through the eyes. You know the upliftment you experience when someone who loves you and whom you love looks at you and through their glance conveys all the love that is present for you. You see refelected to you your potential, your value and your worth. You see a positive vision of yourself that can sustain you and give you the courage and confidence to grow and expand and express more than you've ever dared before.

The power of the gaze is tremendous. When that is coupled with the energy of pure Spirit, it can shake loose levels of your consciousness that have been covered in layers of deception, tradition, convention, rigid expression and other false images. A long time ago, I used to conduct seminars which began with people contributing something of themselves by saying their name and sharing something about themselves with the group. People used to prepare their sharings days in advance, rehearsing just what they would say to sound good. But when they arrived and I looked at them and said, "Okay, next," they would often say something entirely different. Then they would add,"I don't know why I told you that. I wasn't going to say anything about that, but now I'm really glad I did."

The power of the gaze, when used with the Traveler Consciousness, is referred to as the Twaji, an arabic word meaning *the gaze of God.* When that energy is placed toward you, the sincerity of your beingness surfaces, and in spite of any attempt to be deceitful, you hear yourself speaking truth and saying things that are real and present for you. Once you speak the truth, you clear the deceit from within you, and the energy of Spirit anchors with you. Then you can transmit Twaji to others. You may go out and talk to a friend who begins to tell you something, but suddenly tells you something entirely different. The person may say, "I wasn't going to talk about that, but for some reason, I felt it was important to tell you." The gaze of the Traveler has gone through you to the next one. And it will go to the next one and the next and the next. It's a beautiful way to serve Spirit, as it puts people in touch with the truth of their own being.

The power of Spirit promotes and perpetuates total honesty in your consciousness. It is no respector of your dishonesty. Twaji differs somewhat from Darshan, which is the vision of the Light that can bring about a form of spiritual enlightenment. Twaji, the gaze of God presented to you through the Traveler consciousness, can go beyond that in its effect. It can establish you in Soul consciousness immediately. This level of the Twaji is often presented when a person is getting ready to die from the physical level. Twaji is presented, and the person immediately transcends the physical and is established in Spirit.

There are many levels to the energy of Twaji. It can be given in a very powerful and direct way or in the most off-handed way. When you think it's going to happen, it usually doesn't. It happens when it happens; it is nothing you can control or manipulate into being. It rarely happens in a group, although it can. Sometimes when you're sitting in a group with the Traveler and he looks at you, you'll experience something flooding through you — but then he looks away and keeps going with casual conversation because you can't stand any more of the energy than you have received. When you can move into a position of acceptance inside of yourself when you are in the presence of the Traveler, you are opening yourelf to receive Twaji. If you put yourself in positions of defending your point of view, being the "wit" or the "know-it-all," you can block Twaji from coming forward because the energy could impact on your inner resistance and destroy you. It is important to let things flow; it's possible to receive much more if you do not seek to restrict yourself or anyone else, on any level.

I observed another spiritual teacher give Twaji within a group situation where it was done so very fast that the person receiving Twaji blanked out for just a second. It is not unusual for one receiving Twaji to blank out; that leaves the space open for the person to be filled anew with living life. Twaji is like the living waters. You are washed clean, and in that new purity, you actually start hearing the Sound of God as the Sound Current floods through you. It is something you can never forget.

Those who are initiated into the Sound Current of God often experience Twaji during their spiritual exercises. When you see the eyes of the Traveler appear to you inwardly, you are receiving the Twaji inwardly. In that moment, there is no physical form present to corrupt the Spirit, and you enter into freedom. The consciousness of the Traveler is eternally free and gives of its freedom. It gives of its freedom and its love; there is nothing else to give.

As you experience Twaji, you awaken to the Spirit within you, and you move into a new level of responsibility to Spirit. As part of the new responsibility, you must maintain the awareness of Spirit and turn from the negativity of the lower worlds. You must turn away from your hurt, your lust, your greed, and your bad-mouthing. You do this by shifting your attitude. Let me demonstrate this to you. Think of someone right now with whom you were disturbed in your childhood. A teacher? A classmate? A friend? And very quickly, ask yourself how truly important they are in your present life, right now. See how fast the disturbance started leaving you? You couldn't hold it to you. If you try to pull it back to you, it will leave again. You can't hold it. The Twaji, the *Baraka* has come between you and that incident and washed it clean. When you gaze upon *anything* in the Light of God's Spirit, you cannot hold the negative form. You will only be able to hold the positive form. Perhaps, in the moment of letting go of the old disturbance, you saw how it served you and helped you grow. That's the positive form.

Jesus met a Samarian woman at the well, and He asked her some questions. She tried to put Him off and not answer directly. He turned His countenance upon her and she said to Him, "I know that Messiah cometh, which is called Christ: when He is come, He will tell us all things. Jesus saith unto her, 'I that speak unto thee am He'." (John 4:25-26) He revealed His ultimate message to a woman who had had five husbands and was living with a sixth man who was not her husband. He gave the celestial message to a woman. I guess maybe Jesus really started the anti-sexist point of view because, prior to that time, women in the culture had been used for childbearing and all sorts of labor, but were not considered worthy to receive the message of the Christ, the Messiah, the Light of the world.

She not only heard the words of His message, but by His look, the Twaji, she was transformed and made new. She went back into the village and told the men of the village, "Come, see a man, which told me all things that ever I did: is not this the Christ? Then they went out of the city and came unto Him." (John 4:29-30) The gaze of the Master went through her to them, and they all came to Jesus to receive. Do you see your responsibility as a Light bearer? You cannot put forth negativity because you have it wrapped in spiritual energy, and within that is the ability to transform the beingness of another individual. That ability is nothing you can ask for; if the Master gives it to you, you are able to hold it. If it isn't given to you, there is no need to ask. I tell you these things because they are part of spiritual knowledge. You are learning parts now; soon you will know the totality of Spirit as it presents itself to you.

As you gain the discipline to express yourself consistently in honest, forthright ways, you are training yourself to hold the vision of Spirit steady within you. As you do your spiritual exercises or meditation, you bring yourself into alignment with the Spirit. As you conduct yourself in ways which are responsible to yourself and not inflictive on others, you bring yourself into line with spiritual admonitions. Then you can receive the gifts of Spirit. You prepare yourself to have the gaze of God start working in and through you. If you attempt to get the gifts to abuse or take undue advantage of someone else, you will find yourself blocked and frustrated at every turn. If you only wish to serve God, the gifts you can be given are many.

Be steady in your consciousness. As soon as you say, "I'll do this...no, I'd rather do this...no, I think I'll do that..." you have split your consciousness. What do you do to correct the situation? Sit still until the consciousness brings itself together and you see clearly what direction you should take. Do meditation, contemplation, or spiritual exercises as a daily practice. Learn the discipline of consciousness. Hold your gaze steady on your goal. If you are distracted by everything that comes along, you will not reach your goal. Spirit needs those who will move steadily forward.

In the latter days, there will be many who say, "I am the Light, the Truth and the Way." How will you know the one who speaks truly to you? You will know them by their works. If you have disciplined yourself to complete that which you have begun, to treat every person honestly, fairly, and with a loving heart, you will recognize those qualities in others. If you are scattered and inconsistent in your consciousness, your attention will slip, and you will not be able to hold steady long enough to recognize the inconsistencies in others. If you know the discipline of steadiness, you will be able to clearly see when someone else is slipping, and you will not be deceived.

By your works you will be known. You prepare your own feast, and you partake of your own feast. If you delay because you do not recognize your own worthiness, then there is no need to seek elsewhere. If you cannot find God within yourself, you will not find him anywhere else. Until you give yourself awareness of your own beingness, until you are loyal to your own Soul, until you use the Twaji to gaze inwardly, letting it light the path to your own reality, you will not know God. The Traveler teaches of finding the inner Kingdom, of the inner realms of consciousness, of the absoluteness and purity of each individual in Soul. Learn those lessons well. Experience your own divinity. Receive the *Baraka,* the Darshan, the Twaji, and use those qualities to grow in your spiritual knowledge and love. Then you will be able to give those qualities to others.

When you see others, look into their hearts — not to check their levels, but to find the place where you can place your love with them. When you give them love, do not hold onto the other end. Give it and let it go completely. They are free to do with it as they wish. They can share it with anyone or nobody, and you don't care because you have let it go. Don't let anybody buy your allegiance. Give your allegiance freely where you want to give it, but don't demand anything in return. If you do, you've sold yourself short, and are no longer free.

Spirit is given to you freely, and freely you must receive. There is no other way to receive it. You cannot receive Spirit intellectually, emotionally, or physically. You cannot think about it, feel it or touch it. And yet it is more valuable to you than your next breath. It is the living water of life. It is the ocean of divine love and mercy. It is the essence of life itself. In Spirit, there is no time and no space. All exists right now, in eternity. All exists as One. There is no division, no separation. One Soul is all Souls. Jesus said, "He that hath seen me hath seen the Father." (John 14:9) He demonstrated tremendous understanding, seeing Himself through all others. When you realize that you are all things, you also include yourself. The realizations do not come with mentalizing or verbalization; they come from the intelligence of the Soul, from the knowledge inherent within you. Gain the knowledge and the understanding of your Self, and you will be able to live your life from a position of wisdom.

If you want to see clearly, practice the admonitions of the Buddha, of Jesus the Christ, or of any of the great masters. Practice until they are perfect. In perfection, you will be in your Soul because all of these paths eventually lead to the Soul. If you study religion, do it perfectly. If you study metaphysics, do it perfectly. If you study the science of mind, do it perfectly. It will point the way to your next step of fulfillment and completion. As you see the Light, you will experience the Twaji. You will see the Light coming out of your own countenance, your own beingness, and then all you do is follow the Light. Remember to follow the *Source* of the Light, not the reflection. Don't forget that the Source is in you.

After you've completed the pathway you're on, and you see no more Light ahead of you, stop and go within. Recharge the battery. Worship your own beingness, not in selfish love, but in love of Self. Give up all the lower levels and adore, worship, and love the God essence inside of you. All else is reflective and illusory. Spiritual exercises and meditation will point you back to the stability of the spiritual life.

When you think you have to have something out there in the world, stop and ask yourself, "How do I look through the eyes of God to see if that is good for me?" The gaze of God will start appearing within you. The way will appear before you. The Light will go ahead of you, and you will know your direction.

# 4
# Living Divine Essence

Very often when you become involved in spiritual teachings coming from the high, positive realms of God-awareness and you open yourself to that transcendent consciousness we call the Mystical Traveler, Spirit comes forward by means of what orthodox religions call "grace." Jesus said it this way: "For where two or three are gathered together in my name, there I am in the midst of them." (Matthew 18:20) The people Jesus spoke to might not have understood the Sufi word *Baraka,* so he said it another way, but the meaning is the same. In India, the quality of spiritual blessing is also referred to as *Darshan.* It is a quality very similar to *Baraka* transmitted through the eyes from one to another. This essence can be called many names. We know it as divine love, and through divine love we share *Baraka* with each and every one we meet.

When you, in your individual way, tune into that which is divine love, the center where you know goodness dwells, the place where you truly live and express calmly, peacefuly and with love, then your behavior becomes a true representation of the Christ within you. When this process starts, you are opening the portals of your Soul. Awakening to the Soul is not an intellectual process; it's a state of be-ing and doing.

As your expression becomes more closely mat-ched with the inner integrity of your being, you find yourself moving into the Christ of your inner con-sciousness. It's a place which has no description, although it may be the greatest level of reality you have ever known. As you move to that reality, it is like paying your Self a visit. It's like coming home in-side of yourself. The joy, bliss and ecstacy which can come forward from that small visit with your Self can carry you through some very rough spots in your life. Since you dwell primarily in negative ex-istence — on a negative planet, in the negative realms of Light, in a negative body — you find a greater preponderance of negative things to work through. And you find the Lord of negative crea-tion, the Kal power, is present to prove to you that you are becoming worthwhile and surviving the snares and pitfalls of the lower realms.

It may become evident that if you were to at-tempt to reach the inner consciousness by yourself, you would probably be a very long time becoming aware of the Soul or the essence of divinity within you. One who is a wayshower can greatly speed up the process. When you work with a Master who can guide you and assist you on this level and all the higher levels, you allow Spirit to work with you much more intensively. Spirit is like a fresh breeze blowing from Heaven, making all things new and moving you through all the situations of your life in a spirit of love, friendliness, and acceptance.

When situations in your life become difficult or painful, you may lose track of the fact that Spirit is still present in your life. The situation you perceive as negative may be Spirit's blessing as it gives you the opportunity to clear and release certain karmic conditions very rapidly and move into greater strength and freedom. Sometimes people ask me, "John-Roger, as an agent of the Sarmad, as the Mystical Traveler and Preceptor Consciousness, can't you intercede?" There are things which are possible but not permitted. I work from the realms of positive Light, the realms of the pure, spiritual world. I often back off from the negative worlds. The Holy Spirit rarely comes in and overpowers the Kal force or enforces itself in opposition to the Kal power, knowing very well that the Kal force is here to perform a job. It is here to test and strengthen you, to prove to you your own worth. When you do not pass a test of negativity, that fact does not make the test an evil or bad process; it is a process which lets you know you still have work to do in that area. I can bring *Baraka* to your consciousness to assist you in finding the strength and integrity to deal with the situations in your life. I can help awaken you to your own God center so you gain a clear perspective of God's presence in your life and of your part in the divine plan.

When you turn to the Light and Love within you, you may discover your connection with the Mystical consciousness—and at that point, you may be choosing to break the incarnation pattern with which you have been involved. As you move to break the hold of the lower worlds, you may find the forces of negativity "attacking" you in a much more specific way than before, because if you are involved in the conscious and direct pursuit of spiritual transcendence, they must do their job of making sure you learn the lessons necessary for your growth and upliftment. If you hold strong in your purpose, you will experience, even in the midst of the "attack," the perfect spiritual protection which is extended to you through the consciousness of the Mystical Traveler.

Have you ever noticed that negativity strikes primarily in the area of your weakness? It rarely tests you in the field of your strength because in that type of showdown, it will lose. The negative forces know that, and they have a kind of intelligence that will instinctively go for your weak areas. Just about the time you think you've really got an area mastered, the Kal power comes in to make sure you've mastered it. If you have, you're free. If you haven't, you find yourself still bound by the laws of the lower worlds. And even when you pass the tests and prove your spiritual strength, you have to continually exercise those strengths, because if you slip from spiritual attentiveness, you will be found out.

You're never given anything you cannot handle. That's a spiritual law. There may be things which are difficult to handle or which you'd prefer not to handle, or which you'd like to handle better, but there is nothing given to you that you cannot handle. When you are working with the Mystical Traveler, you come under the spiritual protection of the Holy Spirit. The line of the spiritual hierarchy extends through the divine school of the Holy of Holies to the Silent Ones of the Sarmad or God. Our spiritual connection to the Supreme God is very specific and direct. We do not have to rely on words someone spoke thousands of years ago or theories espoused by great teachers of ancient times, although the spiritual teachings of _any_ age can be both valid and valuable. But in our work, we work with the Mystical Traveler as a living Master who is connected directly into the spiritual hierarchy. And in that way, the teachings come alive in our hearts. They are much more than words on a page. The work I do with you is _inner_ much more than it is _outer._ I give you teachings inwardly in the purity of your heart and Soul. The outer words, the books and discourses, are _reflections_ of the inner teachings. These outer reflections serve to awaken you to the inner teachings that are happening within you twenty-four hours a day. They are only the beginning, not the end.

The teachings show you how to live in a rightful, upright way, bypassing levels of deceit, lies, cheating and dishonesty. You don't have to express those negative areas unless you want to remain here in the physical world. If you want to remain *here* on this negative level, all you have to do is give allegiance to lust, anger, avarice, hatred, despair, envy, vanity, and attachment — you will have guaranteed yourself continued life on this plane.

If you would prefer to walk free of the negative worlds and establish yourself in the spiritual realms, there are only a few qualities necessary. The first one is *acceptance.* You have to accept what is so in your life and be honest with it, not pretending it's something it's not or creating fantasies about how you would like it to be. Just accept what is. The second one is *understanding.* You have to seek understanding by understanding yourself. You don't necessarily have to understand everyone else, but it is important to know and understand yourself. The third one is *responsibility.* You have to take responsibility for yourself and your actions on all levels. And the fourth is *cooperation.* Once you accept what is, understand and take responsibility for yourself and your actions, you can start cooperating with all of that. When you *do* cooperate, you discover you're free.

It can be amazing to discover the good Lord didn't put you here on earth to be a beggar. He put you here and said, "This is the way to learn about me..." and showed you a lot of different ways to learn. You can learn through the process of prayer, through loving your family and children, through caring for others, through meditation, through serving others in time of need, through contemplation, and through many other ways. As you learn about God, those things which were mysteries to you become more clear. Because there is nothing that is not God, as you begin to know God, you know all things. All becomes One.

What if the appearance of the Messiah begins with *you* awakening to the God essence inside of you? What if it is discovering that the glory of God resides within you, as well as within all others? Traditionally, the churches have taught that the glory belongs to the Father. And that is true, but it's incomplete. The Father does His work in this world through each one of us, as we do good works. If you, in your everyday life, can allow the Father to do the work of Spirit through you, you will find your life becomes very simple and very joyful. You will be experiencing *Baraka* as it flows through you into the world. You don't have to control it, make it happen, or make any decisions about it. All you have to do is accept it is happening.

In the state of acceptance, you're moving past attachment and desire. It's so easy to talk about acceptance, but not necessarily easy to demonstrate it in your life. Once you can demonstrate that first spiritual law, you're in the game. Then you can call in the quarterback, which is called selectivity, and along with him comes something which is called discernment. You discern that which is available to you and select what will work best for you. You might ask yourself how well you discern what you are bringing to yourself and how well you test the Spirit.

One of the great follies of following any particular spiritual path is the temptation to "play God" by twisting the teachings to say, "I am spiritual, divine, the essence of God," while forgetting to ground those precepts in the context of this physical reality which includes the body, imagination, emotions, mind and unconscious with all their inherent illusions. You don't have to play what you are, and what you are not, you cannot play. There is no need to misrepresent what is going on. You are not God in the sense of the Sarmad or Supreme God. You do carry within you an essence of God, an essence of the Christ consciousness. Outwardly, you are a reflection of the Soul which is in direct contact with God.

Do not inflict what you identify as your spirituality upon other people. Live in simplicity. Live in the truth of your own beingness, and let your actions speak for you. Until you have the *experience* of the inner consciousness and spiritual worlds, what I tell you is nonsense. Non-sense. It makes no sense. And when you have had the experience of transcendental consciousness, you are awakened to a different reality and you know its truth; then there is nothing you have to believe, and you do not have to go on faith. If it sounds like a fairy tale, accept a challenge from me: prove me wrong.

The value of the Mystical Traveler is that it has traversed the realms of Light, extended itself into the physical form, and now uses the physical form to bring you the teachings on a verbal level, explaining to you that there is more to your existence than the three-dimensional figure you misrepresent yourself to be. You are more than your physical expression. The Mystical Traveler also has the ability to reach into the inner consciousness and strengthen your awareness of Soul until you start to feel that movement inside of you. You may say, "Something's going on, I wonder what it could be." And a voice deep within you says, "Yes, yes, it could be...." So you run to the nearest book to read what it could be. The book won't give you the experience, but you can use it to clarify what your experience has been -- if you're lucky enough to get a book by someone who *knows* what's going on. But whatever you read, you must check the information out for yourself, in your own way, in the integrity of your own beingness.

When you begin to awaken to the Soul, you grow spiritually. As you awaken and begin to see yourself in spiritual reality, you will see the many times you have misrepresented, betrayed and confused yourself. You may be tempted to berate yourself and say, "Look how stupid I've been, I can't be worthwhile." But if you can truly open up and allow yourself to perceive yourself *clearly,* without distortion, you'll see yourself as the Master sees you. You'll know your own worthiness and beauty, and in that moment you'll experience *Baraka* and move into great love for yourself. And you'll also experience *Darshan,* which opens your eyes to spiritual reality. If you're not ready, it won't happen. When you're ready, there will be no way you can stop it.

If you're wise, you won't struggle against what is established on this physical level. You'll work *within* it as you seek to gain greater attunement with higher levels of consciousness. Once you are connected to the Mystical Traveler consciousness and agreement is made to work together, the work goes on twenty-four hours a day. The Traveler does not leave you, no matter what you do physically. The presence of that force within you is the main value of the teachings. The words can be found in many places and are spoken by many. However, when you connect to the presence of Spirit inside you, the teachings are given to you inwardly and become an aspect of your experience

If you can always run to some physical body to ask physical questions and get physical answers, you may not learn to tune inwardly and go into the subtle levels of your own conciousness. It is important to reach within yourself to the source of knowledge and strength and to know for yourself what is right to do. On those higher inner levels, you cannot be deceived. Many times you will be placed in a "predicament " which must be solved. If you reach outward for an answer, you can sometimes get an answer that temporarily seems to assist you, but a week or a month later, you may find yourself right back in the same predicament because you did not go *through* it as a process of your learning. You sought a way out of it through someone or something else. So many times the way *out* of something is to go *through* it and gain the greatest awareness available to you.

To move inside to your own spiritual inner awareness is not always easy to do by yourself. But then, you weren't put here by yourself, either. You were put here as part of the body of God, as heir to the kingdom of Heaven. Usually when you are born into the physical body, you slip behind a veil of forgetfulness and forget your heritage. You forget and forget and forget. Then along comes One who has not forgotten, who sees directly into your inner consciousness, to the beauty you are in your Soul, and tells you what it is. And you say, "I know that." I am not telling you anything you do not know; it's just that you may not have remembered it until you heard it stated. Then you have the inner experience which verifies it as truth and reality. It's much more difficult to have the inner experience of Spirit if you're running around in the world lying and cheating and getting into all sorts of trouble. Many times you get the inner experience of your own sacredness by sitting down and detaching yourself from the physical world in a form of meditation, contemplation or spiritual exercises.

When you are going to be involved in spiritual exercises, gather your awareness and focus it where the root of the nose would meet the middle of the forehead. That is the area we call the spiritual eye or the third eye; it will bring your awareness up out of the lower centers of your body, and you will begin to see in a clearer way. You begin to see spiritually, rather than in terms of this world.

**5**

# *An Agent of God*

---

"In the beginning was the Word, and the Word was with God, and the Word was God." (John 1:1) "And the Word was made flesh and dwelt among us." (John 1:14) The Word is the energy of God existing in pure Sound. It is the essence. It is the audible Lifestream and Lightstream. The Mystical Traveler is an agent for this current of Sound as it issues forth from the Supreme God in the pure realms of Light. It is through connection to the Sound Current that you have the opportunity to move back into the heart of God. When you are attuned to the Sound Current, all you have to do is ride the Sound and you will discover its Source, which is God.

On the lower realms of Light, the Sound and Light are mixed with negative energy; in and above the Soul realm, the Sound Current is pure. It is the most delicious melody that sustains you in all things. People ask me what I do when I am experiencing a "problem" in this world. I move back on the Sound Current into the heart of God where there are no problems, only various aspects of experience. And experiences are your measure of growth...so *viva la experience!* Look forward to your next experience so that you may learn more in your awareness of God.

People sometimes say, "Yes, I want to experience the awareness of God. So why do I have to shine shoes?" And I say, "What do you think God is?" They say, "Are you trying to tell me God is a shined shoe?" Perhaps. It's possible that God may be a shined shoe, a rose, a burning bush, a man, a child, all of these things and much, much more. People ask, "Then where will I go to find God?" Go wherever God is. And since God is everywhere, in everything, entirely and eternally present in your breath, you find God by watching and listening. You watch for the Light, both in the physical form and the inner form; you listen for the Sound of God in everything you encounter. When you are watching, both outwardly and inwardly, Spirit will appear to you. It may come to you as *Baraka,* as the awareness of the blessings in your life. It may come as a peace which transcends all understanding. It may come as the Darshan, as your sight is opened to spiritual reality. However you receive Spirit, in that moment, you're going to have a form of a transcendental experience.

If you are not quite in attunement with your own divine essence, if you are not having that experience of _Baraka,_ you may choose to gather with others who seek to know God. Gather together in the name of the Christ, in the consciousness of the Mystical Traveler/Preceptor, in Satsang, or in the consciousness of One. However you identify it, when you are gathering together in God's name, Spirit appears and _Baraka_ is extended to you through the grace of the One God. If you come together and decide to do your own ego trip, you weaken the _Baraka_ which would have been extended to you, and you may become out of balance with your own divine consciousness.

When those who can manifest _Baraka_ bring it forward into a gathering, the blessings are bestowed instantly on all present. If divine essence is brought to you, and you do not partake of it and step forward into divine love, you deny the Holy Spirit. To deny this experience is serious on the spiritual levels, but only inasmuch as you block yourself from the reality of your own knowing. Other than that, Spirit doesn't care whether you remain on this plane for two thousand years or one day. If you discover the reality which IS, you have completed the lesson of this earthly "classroom" and are able to transcend to another experience.

It is interesting that the ancient law governing bestowal of _Baraka_ states that it must be done by a physical presence. Once the physical presence has bestowed or activated this essence of divine energy, those who have received *Baraka* can, in turn, bestow it on others. The more you receive of it, the more you can give it to others. This is how you have the authority to do God's work.

It is by your works you are known, not by your mouth. A lot of people say a lot of things, but are not capable of delivering divine essence, and it is that *ability* which is important. It is the reason we meet and come together to open up the channels which can receive of the essence of Spirit. That part which receives of Spirit is so vast that we could meet together for a millenium and never become satiated.

No one who has experienced *Baraka* and maintained a consciousness which is open to the flow of *Baraka* will feel the negativity of this planet to any great extent. As long as you are open, letting the love flow and directing your Light out, you are receiving and giving of *Baraka,* the Holy Spirit, the Light and Sound. You are an instrument of Light. The Spirit uses you to bring Light into this physical realm, and it radiates from you to all others on this level. You receive *Baraka,* and you, in turn, extend *Baraka* to all you meet. You lift your brothers and sisters by your presence and by your Light. No matter what they say or do, no matter what happens, you still function as a channel for the Spirit, to be used or abused; it matters very little either way.

If you are abused, the Light handles that. If you are used, the Light handles that. All you have to do is keep freedom in your consciousness and be open to let Light and love flow through you to everything. You don't have to say, "God bless that flower, that ant, that cockroach, those toadstools, that tree." The blessings come automatically, as soon as Spirit uses you as a channel into the planet. However, if you do take your consciousness and direct it toward a rose bush, if you love it and bless it, it will bear more abundantly. If you pray over seeds with your love, saying, "I will plant you, and you will grow and be magnificent," it will stir the life force within the seed and give it the promise to fulfill.

Human beings grow in awareness in a similar way. God uses us with one another as instruments of Light. Being together in God's name, in the divine love of Spirit, becomes a prayer. You are a walking prayer, even if you say nothing, because Spirit knows your needs. It knows your desires and your wants, too, and will fulfill them according to your awareness. It will not violate your consciousness; it will sustain the energy within you and give you the ability to continually lift into higher and greater awareness.

Those of you who work with the Mystical Traveler consciousness are offered the Holy Spirit. _Baraka_ is extended to you. If you recognize what you have, it enhances your Spirit. If you don't recognize it, your Spirit still sleeps. The Light is given to you consciously; it stirs the intellect and the Soul into recollection of what it really is, its promise and destiny. Then it is up to you to have the wit to look into your own consciousness and see the Light and love. You will see the portals and the keys to the Kingdom of Heaven.

The pathway is being opened for you. The place is being prepared. You're helping to build it. Later you will know it more completely, when your consciousness is stronger, more dedicated, more devoted. Then you can say, "I don't care what it takes. I'm going to find the Spirit. I'm just going to do it. My depression can be a stepping stone for me. My doubt can be a stepping stone. I don't have to stumble on these things; I can use them to my advantage." When you reach that point in your consciousness, you can begin moving into the higher realms of Spirit.

Don't get so caught up in thinking you know everything that you deny the truth which is all around you. There is truth everywhere. There is Light everywhere. The Sound of God is everywhere. But it just so happens that the master forces working with MSIA® do have the keys and techniques to liberate you in your consciousness while you're still in the physical body. But the fact that we can awaken you to that awareness does not mean others cannot also do that.

One key to liberation is eternal vigilance. Salvation is a daily job, a nightly job, an eternal job. If you enter into spiritual discipline and gain a certain level of awareness, you are responsible for that expansion, and you are responsible for continuing it. You cannot stop and "rest on your laurels." It doesn't work that way. You keep going. We sometimes talk about being on a spiritual path, but that's a misnomer, for there is no path. There is no distance. There is no "end" to this discovery. You are already all that you will be. You are already that which you seek. The *blessings already are,* and all you need to do is open your eyes and see that. All you need is the realization.

The keys to realization are in the Mystical Traveler consciousness, not in the words I speak or write, but in the consciousness itself. The verbal or written level is only a part of the ten percent level of physical manifestation. Ninety percent of your beingness lives in the invisible levels around and within you. The spiritual levels go on and on. They are infinite and eternal. Just because you don't perceive them doesn't mean they are not present. You don't perceive radio waves, either, until you turn on the radio and channel that reality into you. In a similar way, you may not be aware of "spiritual rays" until you have an instrument to measure them. You have that instrument; you *are* that intrument. But you may not have "tuned yourself" to receive Spirit. Part of my work is to teach you how to attune yourself to the Spiritual rays which are present. One of the ways I do that is to present spiritual energy to you continuously. As you receive that spiritual energy, it awakens the spiritual energy in you. Then the changes happen from the inside out.

The Mystical Traveler consciousness, as an agent of God, draws its energy from the pure, spiritual realms. God is the greatest level of reality you can experience. It is pure Light and Sound. It is the Source. It is not image or reflection or illusion. It is the only reality. That reality exists within you also. It is your Soul. You can drop all the illusions, images, facades. You can go within and find that which is real within you. You can discover God dwelling within. As you move to that awareness, you experience the grace of God in your life. You experience Darshan, the clear sight. You experience the Twaji, the gaze of God which lifts you into the high realms of Soul consciousness. You experience _Baraka,_ the essence of divine love.

If you attempt to reconcile in your mind the seeming paradox of God in the flesh and God in the invisible realms, you will falter and fall into your own doubt, confusion, and despair. Some churches call it sin, but it's mostly despair. Grab yourself by the bootstraps. Forgive yourself for the confusions and disturbances you've perpetrated against yourself. Resolve to take your next breath in love. Resolve to breath in God in your next breath. You're breathing the same air that Jesus the Christ, Buddha, Krishna, Muhammad and all the other great spiritual teachers and leaders of all times breathed. With each breath you can awaken yourself to greater and greater spiritual awareness. Practice spiritual exercises. Practice seeing the Light. Practice hearing the Sound. Practice seeing yourself through the eyes of the Master. Practice the Mystical Traveler consciousness.

You don't have to go very far to be in Heaven; The Spirit is nearer than your own hands and feet. You are already that which you wish to be. You are already Light. You are already the divine perfection in your Soul. You are already love. You are already peace. All I say to you is, "Let's go. There is a place prepared for you in Heaven." *No man comes to me that I will not lift him.* These, too, can be the words you pray and the consciousness you demonstrate. No man will come to me that I do not radiate to him something of the greatness of the Spirit, of divine love and Light, of *Baraka.* This, too, you can do. These things are of greater service to mankind than I can express in words. These things simply are.

My peace I give to you because I have peace, and my love I give to you because I have love. I give you to you because I am all. I am everlasting, Alpha and Omega. I am the eternal Now, the manna that falls from heaven. I am the Mystical Traveler and Preceptor. I am self-realized and all is here for me, right now, in this moment. And because I am these things, and because you and I are one, you are these things also.

My realization may be greater at this point in time, but that is the only difference between your consciousness and mine. Through *Baraka* we are one, and all is shared NOW. We say together, "Father, I am so happy for my knowledge of you. I will use my awareness for Thy glory alone because I am your instrument. Whatever I do, I do in your name. I do all things in God's name, with the inner Master to work with me and guide me." As you experience and express your divinity, the shackles of bondage fall away, karma dissolves, and you step into those heavenly planes where the great Masters

of Light are waiting to welcome you home to that
which is your heritage.

Baruch Bashan ·

the Blessings *all ready* are


John-Roger

# ABOUT THE AUTHOR

John-Roger is the spiritual director of the Movement of Spiritual Inner Awareness,[T.M.] or MSIA® . He began his teaching in the late 1950's and incorporated MSIA® in 1971 – now a state and federally recognized Church incorporated in California, New York, Minnesota, Florida, Pennsylvania and Oregon as well as in Great Britain. He is also President of Koh-E-Nor University, Prana Theological Seminary and College of Philosophy, and Golden Age Education, Inc., and an active catalyst/director for INSIGHT Training Seminars, a division of Golden Age Education, Inc. Through these organizations, J-R has conducted literally thousands of seminars and has touched the lives of many thousands of people throughout the world.

John-Roger's taped seminars are offered throughout the United States as well as in Australia, Nigeria, England and France. In the United States, a complete listing of seminars and times is available through the Movement Newspaper, P.O.Box 19458, Los Angeles, CA 90010, (213) 737-1134

John Deanshaw, 25 Glenhaven Road, Glenhaven NSW 2154, Australia 02-634-2445

Chike Madegbuna, 11 Nzegwu Ave.,
P.O. Box 172, Onitsha, Nigeria, West Africa,
046-212-336

Natalie Franks, 102 Clive Ct., Maida-Vale, London, England W91SF

Jean-Georges Henrotte, 11 rue de la Ferronnerie, 75001 Paris, France, 2614036

---

*Soul Awareness Discourses,* offered through the Movement of Spiritual Inner Awareness,[T.M.] are one way John-Roger has chosen to communicate the spiritual teachings as he perceives them.

One discourse each month, offering keys to an uplifting and joyous life. A spiritual notebook to record your progress, dreams and thoughts. A direct, personal connection with John-Roger and the consciousness he holds.

For information on how to subscribe to Soul Awareness Discourses, write to:
MSIA®, P.O.Box 3935, Los Angeles, CA 90051

# BOOKS BY JOHN-ROGER

| Title | Order# | Donation |
| --- | --- | --- |
| A Consciousness of Wealth | | |
| Creating a Money Magnet | 951-3 | $3.00 |
| Awakening Into Light | 975-0 | $3.50 |
| The Christ Within | 959-5 | $3.00 |
| The Consciousness of Soul | 968-8 | $3.50 |
| Disciples of Christ | 955-6 | $2.50 |
| Dream Voyages | 952-1 | $9.00 |
| Drugs | 953-X | $3.00 |
| Dynamics of The Lower Self | 959-9 | $3.00 |
| Inner Worlds of Meditation | 977-7 | $3.50 |
| Journey of a Soul | 967-X | $3.50 |
| Master Chohans | | |
| of the Color Rays | 956-4 | $6.50 |
| Path to Mastership | 957-2 | $5.00 |
| Sex, Spirit and You | 962-9 | $3.50 |
| The Sound Current | 958-0 | $2.50 |
| The Spiritual Family | 978-5 | $3.50 |
| What Is The Power Within You? | 976-9 | $3.50 |
| The Way-Out Book | 998-X | $8.00 |
| Signs of the Times | 948-3 | $7.00 |

John-Roger's teachings are also available on cassettes of the seminars he has given all over the world. To order any of the above, or for a catalog of John-Roger's books and tapes, please write to:
MSIA®,  P.O. Box 3935, Los Angeles, CA 90051

*World economics may change suggested donations.*